HOW THE HEART FEELS

A COLLECTION OF NARRATIVES

AARAV ANAND

To every soul that has ever felt lost, broken, or unseen,
This book is for you.

May these words remind you that your emotions are valid, your struggles are shared, and your heart is stronger than you believe.

And to those who have been the light in the darkest moments of someone, thank you for showing them way forward. This book exists because of you.

Contents

Foreword

Life is a journey marked by countless emotions, each leaving its imprint on the heart. We all experience moments of joy, sorrow, doubt, and resilience, yet the depths of these emotions often remain unspoken. In How My Heart Feels, you are invited to explore the raw, unfiltered truths of the human heart—a mirror to your own experiences, fears, and hopes.

This collection of narratives doesn't shy away from pain or struggle. Instead, it embraces them, offering a space where vulnerability is met with understanding and where brokenness becomes a step toward healing. Each story is a reflection of the quiet battles we face, the thoughts we often hide, and the universal desire to feel seen, valued, and whole.

As you read these pages, you may find yourself revisiting moments of your own life. Let these stories be a companion, a reminder that you are not alone in your feelings. Whether you are searching for solace, understanding, or simply a moment to breathe, this book offers a space for all that your heart holds.

Take this journey one page at a time. Feel deeply, reflect honestly, and most importantly, remember this: every emotion you carry is a part of what makes you beautifully human.

Preface

The heart is a fragile yet powerful part of who we are. It feels deeply, loves unconditionally, and endures pain in ways words often fail to capture. This collection of narratives, How the Heart Feels, is a reflection of the many emotions that shape us, grief, doubt, loneliness, rejection, and more. Each piece dives into the raw and unfiltered reality of what it means to be human, exploring the struggles we often carry in silence.

This book is not just about the pain but also about the quiet strength that emerges when we allow ourselves to feel. It's about finding light in darkness, purpose in chaos, and hope even when it feels impossible. These narratives are meant to resonate with anyone who has ever felt broken, unseen, or lost, offering a reminder that you are not alone in your journey.

As you turn these pages, my hope is that you find comfort in these words and courage in your heart. This is not just a collection of stories, it is a companion for the moments when your soul feels heavy and a reminder that even in the depths of despair, there is always a way forward.

Preface

Acknowledgements

Writing How My Heart Feels has been an emotional journey, one that would not have been possible without the support, guidance, and inspiration of many people.

First and foremost, I want to thank my family, whose unwavering love and encouragement have been my greatest source of strength. You have been my anchor during the toughest of times and my cheerleaders in moments of doubt.

To my friends, thank you for listening, for understanding, and for reminding me of the beauty in connection. Your presence has been a reminder that even in loneliness, I am never truly alone.

A heartfelt thanks to every teacher and mentor who has nurtured my love for writing. Your belief in my voice has given me the courage to share these stories.

Finally, to every soul who picks up this book, thank you. Whether you are here seeking comfort, understanding, or simply a reminder that your emotions matter, I am grateful to share this journey with you. This book exists because of the universal truth that we all feel deeply, and in that, we are connected.

With all my heart,

Aarav

Prologue

Sometimes, a few life pains feel like a carved hole in our hearts, be it losing a loved one or thinking about the harsh words of someone really close to us leaving a hollow hole that can never be filled. Sometimes you feel that life is too much. Thinking about the silent tears and the unfelt pain, this book is a reflection of how the heart feels when life takes you hard. When goodbyes come early, when pain becomes unbearable and when tears become the loss of blood, when the heartache becomes deep and when the shadows become dark, we take life hard on us. This is a collection of stories of love that slipped through my fingers, of words that pierced deeper than any wound, and of the loneliness that follows in the quiet moments after. These are the emotions that haunt us, the memories that cling to our souls, and the tears that never stop falling. It's a glimpse into the raw, aching truth of how the heart truly feels. That look for your inner-self, that night of pain and that feeling of looking outside the window, tired, exhausted of life, is what are known as the stages of life. But that shattered, empty hole can never be replaced.

CHAPTER ONE

THE WINDOW THAT FEELS ME

The screams, the tears, the groans and the tiredness on the face, sitting beside the window with knees touching the chest, looking towards the glamorring cars, the reflective sea and the red blooded moon. Just sitting, with tears, with a broken apart mind begging for a break. Looking over a silent world but on the inside, the heart was screaming.

The unstoppable sobs that shake the body. Every breath feels heavy, like the weight of the pain carries is too much to bear. Whispering into the empty room, "Please help... take me away!" begging for a break—just one moment where life doesn't hurt so much. But no one hears. It's just the heart, the soul and the darkness, with a feeling like the world has forgotten the soul's existence.

It's hard to explain this kind of pain, the kind that lingers in your bones, the kind that makes you feel like you're breaking from the inside out. It's the pain of a heart that's been shattered too many times, of dreams that have slipped through the fingers like sand. It's the kind of pain that makes you question if you can keep going, if you even want to.

The closing of eyes, wishing the soul could just disappear into the night, fade into the shadows where the hurt can't find it. But no matter how hard the tries are to escape it, the pain is always there, like an unwelcome companion that refuses to leave. The soul doesn't know how to make it stop. The soul doesn't know if it ever will.

The last look out the window one last time, searching the sky for something—hope, a sign, anything to tell that this won't last forever. But all it could see was darkness. The stars, once so bright and full of promise, seem dim and far away. And the soul left here, alone with the thoughts, the tears, and the unbearable weight of a heart that feels like it's breaking beyond repair.

Not knowing how much more can be taken. Everything feels too hard, too heavy, too much. Just wanting the pain to stop, for the tears to dry, and for the heart to heal. But at this moment, it feels like that will never happen. So the soul just sits by the window, crying, waiting, hoping for something , anything, that will make this exhaustion end until the light dims and the blackness grows.

CHAPTER TWO

BEING ALONE

There is a kind of loneliness that goes deeper than simply being alone. It's the feeling of standing in a crowded room and yet feeling invisible, like no one sees you, no one understands the heart. The world moves on, people laugh, talk, and go about their lives, but the soul feels like its standing alone, as if separated by an invisible wall. No one notices the quiet sadness, the empty silence that fills each day.

There is a heaviness to it, a sense that no one truly sees, no one truly understands.

Sitting alone in a room, watching others talk from a distance, hearing laughter that doesn't include you. The soul begins to wonder if its invisible, if there is something missing, something that makes it different, somehow less deserving of connection. It's hard to shake the feeling that maybe this isolation is its own doing, that maybe there is something wrong, something that pushes people away.

CHAPTER THREE

Going Back with Guilt

Guilt is your shadow, always following you and reminding you of the moments that you feel you can go back to and just change everything. Guilt is a heavy feeling that fills you with regret and shame, wanting you to hide yourself from others and being alone. There were words that should not have been said, choices that hurt others, actions that left scars. Each time the soul thinks back, there is a twist of pain, a feeling of regret that just doesn't fade.

The soul wonders why it couldn't have done things differently. It asks itself over and over,"Why did I act like that? How could I have hurt someone who trusted me?" These questions haunt the quiet moments, filling the soul with sadness and shame. Guilt is a feeling of anger and shame. The soul feels sad about what happened but also angry at itself for causing harm. And as much as the soul wants to forget, the memories stay clear, playing back as if it happened only yesterday.

Each memory feels sharp, like its punishing the soul, reminding it of the hurt it caused. But after a while, the soul begins to understand that it can't stay trapped in this pain forever. Holding onto guilt only makes the heart heavier, and life feels harder to live. Slowly, the soul tries to make peace with what happened. It realizes that everyone makes mistakes, that even good people sometimes hurt others without meaning to.

The guilt won't disappear in a day, but the soul starts to believe that it deserves a chance to heal. Little by little, the soul learns to forgive itself. It remembers that what matters most is trying to be better, to not repeat the same mistakes. The past cant be changed, but the soul finds a new strength in moving forward, choosing to carry the lesson, not the pain. And as it goes on, the weight of guilt becomes lighter, turning into a reminder of growth and a step toward becoming whole again.

CHAPTER FOUR

SILENT SCREAMS OF REJECTION

Rejection feels like a sharp, unexpected cut. It is the feeling of putting yourself out there, hoping to be accepted, only to be met with silence, with a closed door. It is a pain that goes deep, making the soul feel unworthy, like it wasn't enough. The soul takes everything on itself that it wasn't deserving enough to be accepted. It questions itself on its abilities and wondering if it is flawed.

At first, rejection feels like a failure, a dialogue said by the heart that "you are not enough, you never will be!" The soul wants itself to be invisible, hidden from others, hidden from its own shadows. There is an emptiness in rejection, a hollow feeling that seems to echo. The soul remembers all the effort it put in, all the hopes it held onto, only for it all to come crashing down. Every detail replays in the mind the words that were spoken, the looks that were given, the way things ended.

The mind clings to these memories, almost as if they are proof of its own shortcomings. It is easy to fall into a spiral, to believe that the rejection is a sign that something is wrong, that maybe the soul is truly unworthy. In those first moments, the soul can feel trapped, unable to see beyond the pain. It tries to find answers, to make sense of why things didn't go as hoped. Maybe it thinks it wasn't good enough, that there was something it could have done better, something it could have changed.

It is hard to shake the feeling that if only it had been smarter, kinder, or more talented, things would be different. But as the soul reflects more deeply, a quiet truth starts to take shape. It realizes that no one is perfect, that rejection isn't always a reflection of who it is or what it deserves. People are complex, circumstances are unpredictable, and sometimes, even the best efforts don't lead to the outcome we hope for.

The soul slowly begins to understand that rejection is not a measure of its value. It is not a final judgment on who it is or what it has to offer. Rejection is, in fact, a part of life's journey, something that everyone experiences in one form or another. It is a common thread in the human story, a challenge that teaches resilience, understanding, and even a new way to see the world. Over time, the soul finds a different perspective. It seems that rejection doesn't mean its unlovable or broken.

It simply means that this particular path wasn't the one it was meant to walk. There is freedom in this understanding a sense that rejection is not the end but rather a redirection, a nudge to look elsewhere, to open up to new possibilities. It is not easy, and the pain of rejection doesn't disappear overnight. But the soul begins to see that each no doesn't erase its worth. Instead, it's a stepping stone on a longer path, one that is filled with lessons, with growth, with chances to become stronger.

With time, the soul begins to build a quiet confidence. It starts to believe in its own worth, not because others validate it, but because it starts to see the good within itself. The soul learns to stand tall, even in moments of doubt. It realizes that it doesn't need the approval of everyone to feel valuable; its worth is already there, waiting to be seen and embraced. Each time it faces rejection, it hurts, yes, but it hurts a little less, and the sting becomes a reminder that it is still here, still moving forward, still capable of giving and receiving love. As days turn into weeks, and weeks into months, the soul learns to trust that the right people, the right opportunities will come along when the time is right. It learns that sometimes, the best things in life arrive after facing setbacks and disappointments.

Slowly, the soul lets go of the idea that it needs to be perfect, that it needs to be accepted by everyone to feel whole. Instead, it embraces itself, flaws and all, seeing each part of itself as worthy, as enough.

This journey is not an easy one. There are days when rejection still stings deeply, when old fears creep back in, whispering that maybe it will always be alone, always be left behind. But even on those days, there is a newfound strength, a resilience that wasn't there before. The soul has learned to keep going, to believe in itself even when others don't, to find comfort in its own presence.

Rejection, once so painful, has now become just one chapter in a larger story, a story that holds new beginnings, unexpected turns, and the promise of a future that is still unfolding. The soul moves forward, carrying the lessons of each rejection, trusting that it will find its way, that it will continue to grow, to heal, and to discover new paths, new dreams, new chances to become whole. Rejection has shaped it, but it does not define it. Its just one part of a story that is still being written, one that will lead to places the soul has yet to imagine.

CHAPTER FIVE

DOUBTING SELF

Doubting oneself feels like standing on shaky ground, unsure if the next step will hold or crumble beneath the weight. The soul wrestles with constant questions, "Am I good enough? What if I fail? What if they see that I don't belong?" The thoughts swirl endlessly, like a storm that refuses to calm. No matter how much effort is given, the soul feels as if It's never enough, as if its always falling short of some unseen standard.

The doubt doesn't need a reason to exist, it just does, creeping in during moments of silence, whispering that success is a fluke, that every achievement is luck, that failure is just waiting around the corner. It pulls the soul into a spiral of second guessing, turning even the simplest decisions into battles between fear and hope. Each time the soul looks in the mirror, it sees flaws others might not notice, hears criticisms no one has spoken, feels the weight of expectations no one has set.

It becomes exhausting, carrying the burden of proving worth to others, to itself, and failing to feel that worth even when it's earned. The soul begins to believe the doubts as if they are truths, letting them shape its actions, its thoughts, its sense of identity. Self-doubt is isolating. Even when others offer reassurance, the soul struggles to believe them.

Compliments are brushed off as politeness, success is diminished as luck, and the soul wonders if its only a matter of time before others see the flaws it feels are so obvious. The fear of being exposed as not enough lingers, like a shadow that follows every step. Over time, the soul starts to realize that doubt is not a reflection of truth but of fear, fear of failure, fear of judgment, fear of not living up to what it hopes to be.

It's a hard truth to face because doubt feels safe in its own way. It keeps the soul cautious, keeps it from taking risks. But it also keeps the soul small, chained to the belief that it can't do more, be more. The journey out of self-doubt is slow, filled with steps forward and steps back. The soul begins to understand that doubting itself doesn't mean its incapable; it means its human. Every person carries doubt in some form, even those who seem confident and strong.

The soul starts to see that doubt can be challenged not by waiting for it to disappear, but by acting in spite of it. Little by little, the soul learns to trust itself. It celebrates small wins, finding courage in the tiniest victories. It reminds itself that perfection isn't the goal and that mistakes don't define worth. The doubts don't vanish overnight, and some days, they come back stronger than ever.

But with each step forward, the soul grows stronger, finding proof in its own actions that it is capable, that it can rise above the fears. Self-doubt may always linger, but the soul no longer lets it take the lead. Instead, it becomes a quiet companion, one that reminds the soul to stay humble, to keep striving, but never to stop believing in its own potential. The soul moves forward, not because the doubts are gone, but because it knows that strength isn't the absence of doubt it is the courage to move forward anyway.

CHAPTER SIX

MOVING ON

Moving on feels like betrayal. The soul knows it's necessary, that life demands it, but the guilt clings tightly, refusing to let go. Memories of what was of people, places, and moments linger, reminding the soul of what it's leaving behind. It feels like you're erasing a part of yourself, as if moving forward means forgetting the love, the laughter, the pain that shaped you.

The soul wonders if it is selfish to want more, to seek happiness when the past still calls. It is a tug-of-war between the need to grow and the fear of losing touch with what once defined you. With time, the soul learns that moving on doesn't mean forgetting. It doesn't mean the love wasn't real or that the pain wasn't valid. It means carrying those memories with you, not as chains, but as pieces of a larger story. Moving on is not an end, it is a continuation, a step toward finding peace.

CHAPTER SEVEN

WANTING TIME

Time slips away quietly, unnoticed until its gone. The soul looks back and sees moments it let slip through its fingers opportunities missed, relationships neglected, dreams not left pursued. There is a deep sadness in realizing how much was lost, how much was left undone. The soul begins to feel trapped in the weight of "What if. What if it had tried harder? What if it had been braver?" These questions haunt the quiet moments, filling the soul with regret.

But as the soul sits with this grief, it begins to see that even wasted time carries lessons. It learns to cherish the moments ahead, to make the most of what remains. The past cannot be changed, but the future is still unwritten, waiting for the soul to step forward.

CHAPTER EIGHT

NOT BEING THANKED

There is a quiet hurt in giving your all and feeling it go unnoticed. The soul pours its energy, it's time, it is love into others, into work, into life itself, only to be met with silence. No acknowledgment, no gratitude, just an emptiness that makes every effort feel invisible. It starts as a small sting, a fleeting thought, "Did they not notice? Did it not matter?"

But as the days pass and the silence continues, that sting deepens into a wound. The soul begins to wonder if its efforts are in vain, if It's destined to give endlessly without receiving anything in return. The pain isn't just about recognition, it is about wanting to feel seen, to feel valued. Every human craves to know that what they do matters, that their presence leaves a mark, even in small ways.

Without that acknowledgment, the soul starts to question its worth. It begins to shrink, to doubt, to wonder if it should even bother trying any more. But even in this darkness, the soul learns an important truth: appreciation cannot always come from others. Sometimes, it must come from within. Slowly, it begins to acknowledge its own efforts, to celebrate the quiet victories no one else sees. It learns to take pride in its work, in its love, in its perseverance, even when others don't.

The soul discovers that being unappreciated does not mean it is unworthy. It finds strength in knowing that its value isn't tied to others recognition but to the simple fact that it exists, that it tries, that it continues despite the silence. And in this, the soul begins to heal, carrying forward with the quiet, unshakable belief that one day, someone will see, someone will notice, someone will truly appreciate the light it brings. Until then, the soul learns to be its own source of gratitude.

CHAPTER NINE

IT'S NOT THE SAME

The world feels empty now. The soul feels broken, as if a piece of it is missing and nothing can make it whole again. Losing someone you love leaves an ache so deep, it's like a weight pressing down on the chest, making it hard to breathe, hard to move, hard to even think. They are gone, and nothing feels the same. Everywhere, there are reminders. Their favourite chair, their old sweater left on the bed, the way their voice used to fill the room. The soul reaches out for them, longing to hear that voice, to feel that warmth, but there is only silence. A silence that feels heavy and cold, a silence that reminds the soul, again and again, that they are not coming back. The memories come, one by one, like tiny waves crashing over and over. The sound of their laughter, the way they would say, It's going to be okay, the gentle look in their eyes that could make the world feel safe.

The soul clings to these memories, but they hurt now, too. Each memory is like a spark of light in the darkness, yet each one reminds the soul of the emptiness that is left behind. Grief is a pain that goes so deep, it feels like it touches every part of the soul. It feels like a weight that can never be lifted, a sadness that has no end. Days go by, but nothing feels better. The world keeps moving, but the soul feels trapped in a moment that can't be escaped, a moment of pure, aching loss.

Sometimes, it feels like a bad dream, like any minute they will walk back into the room, and this empty feeling will just vanish.

But they don't come back. And the soul feels a pain so sharp It's hard to even cry. There's only a hollow space inside, where love and happiness used to be. Some days, the soul just wants to say one last goodbye. Just one last chance to hold their hand, to look them in the eyes and say, "You meant everything to me. I love you, and I always will." But that chance is gone now.

The soul is left with words that have no place to go, love that has nowhere to rest. There are nights when the soul lies awake, feeling the weight of everything that will never be. No more shared laughter, no more talks, no more hugs. Just the memories, which are beautiful but also painful, because they are only memories now. And the soul feels a loneliness that's hard to explain this loneliness that is as wide and endless as the sky, but so empty it feels like it could consume everything

The tears come, soft at first, then harder, as if all the pain is finally pouring out. Each tear feels like a small piece of the soul breaking away, a release of all the love that has nowhere else to go. The soul cries not only for the person who is gone but for every dream, every hope, every future moment that will never happen. The tears are endless, and yet they feel like the only way to hold on.

The soul wishes there was a way to reach them, a way to send love across the distance. Maybe they can still hear, maybe they know. But it is not the same. Nothing will ever be the same. And slowly, very slowly, the soul begins to understand that this pain is here to stay. The love remains, but now it lives in a different forma form that brings both warmth and sorrow. The soul learns that grief is simply love that has nowhere to go, love that must now live on in memories, in thoughts, in whispers.

In time, the soul may find peace, not because the pain is gone, but because it has become part of who it is. The ache will stay, but with it comes a quiet strength, a reminder that love is so powerful, so deep, that not even death can erase it. And in that, the soul finds a reason to keep going, to carry their memory forward, knowing that a part of them will always be there, held close forever, in a place only love can reach.

The Heartbreak

Heartbreak isn't just pain, its emptiness. It is the feeling of loving someone so deeply that they become a part of you, only to lose them and feel that part of yourself disappear. The soul feels hollow, like everything it held close has vanished, leaving only a silent, aching space. Every thought turns back to them, replaying words, moments, laughter, as if searching for something missed, as if hoping there's still a way to make things right. The sadness doesn't just sit in the heart, it fills the entire body, a kind of numbness that makes everything feel gray, distant, like a fog that won't lift. Days pass, but the pain remains, constant and familiar, a reminder of the love that once felt like it would last forever. Each place, each song, each familiar sight feels like a reminder of what has been lost, of a connection that was once so full of warmth and joy but is now only a memory. The hardest part is accepting that they are truly gone, that the dreams once shared are now only echoes in the mind. The soul tries to let go, but It's hard to release something that felt so real, so right. It feels impossible to imagine life without them, to imagine moving forward when every step feels like its leaving them further behind. The world feels quiet, muted, as if joy itself has been dimmed, as if happiness is something that only belongs in the past.But somehow, in the quietest moments, a small glimmer of hope begins to emerge, a reminder that love, even if lost, leaves a mark that cannot be erased. The love remains, a part of the soul that grows stronger with time, that allows the heart to heal while holding onto what was beautiful. It's a slow journey, but in time, the soul learns to carry the love with peace, finding strength in the memory, a gentle acceptance that allows it to move forward, carrying the love as part of itself.

Realizing

Loss is a wound that feels like it will never heal. The soul feels empty, broken, as if a piece of it has been ripped away. But even in this deep pain, there is a way forward not to erase the loss, but to learn to live with it. The first step is allowing yourself to grieve. Cry if you need to, scream if you must. Let the pain flow instead of holding it in. Suppressing grief only makes the wound deeper. The soul needs to feel the sorrow to begin healing.

Slowly, the soul learns to cherish memories instead of fearing them. Those moments, the ones that once brought joy, are not gone. They are still alive in your heart. Talk about the person, remember their laughter, their kindness. Keep their spirit alive in the way you live your own life. And while the void will never completely disappear, it becomes a part of who you are, reminder of love, of connection, of the beauty of caring so deeply.

Over time, the soul learns to carry this love forward, to honour what was lost by continuing to live, even when it feels impossible.

CHAPTER TEN

OVERCOMING THOUGHTS

Life often feels overwhelming, filled with loss, doubt, loneliness, and moments of feeling unseen. These emotions can weigh heavily on the soul, making it question its worth, its direction, and its place in the world. But even in the darkest moments, healing and strength are possible. The first step is acceptance. Whether its grief from loss, the ache of loneliness, or the sting of rejection, the soul must allow itself to feel.

Suppressing these emotions only deepens the wounds. Cry if you need to, seek comfort in trusted people, or spend time with yourself in quiet reflection. Feeling the pain is not weakness, it is the beginning of healing. With time, the soul learns that it is stronger than it seems. Loss teaches the value of love, doubt challenges the soul to grow, loneliness offers a chance to connect deeply with oneself, and rejection reveals paths not yet seen.

Overcoming these struggles doesn't mean they vanish; it means the soul grows resilient. Slowly but surely, it learns to find purpose and light again, building a life filled with meaning, even after pain.

Life Makes The Going Tough

“*"Life's struggles test the heart in ways that can feel unbearable. Loss makes it ache, doubt clouds its path, and loneliness creates emptiness. Rejection hurts, making it feel unworthy. Yet through every hardship, the heart learns to heal. With time, it grows stronger, more resilient, and finds the courage to love again. The heart may break, but it never loses its ability to rise, learn, and find peace even in the face of pain."*”

This quote reflects how life's challenges, such as loss, doubt, loneliness, and rejection can deeply hurt the heart. However, despite these painful experiences, the heart has the strength to heal, grow stronger, and continue to find hope and love. It emphasizes resilience and the ability to rise above difficulties.